WALKS WITH CHILDREN
IN THE
LAKE DISTRICT:

BORROWDALE

Other *Questa* Guides, published and
in production

Walks with Children in the Lake District:
Buttermere and the Vale of Lorton
Patterdale
Ambleside and Grasmere
Around Coniston
Keswick and the Newlands Valley

Walks with Children in the New Forest
Walks with Children in the Peak District
Around Hathersage
Edale and Castleton
Walks with Children in the West Country
South Devon and Dartmoor

WALKS with CHILDREN
in the Lake District
BORROWDALE

Terry Marsh

A Questa Guide

© Terry Marsh 1994
ISBN 1 898808 05 8

Questa Publishing
27 Camwood, Clayton Green, Bamber Bridge
PRESTON, Lancashire, PR5 8LA

ADVICE TO READERS

Readers are advised that while the author has take every
effort to ensure the accuracy of this guidebook, and has
been required to revisit all the routes during the course of
preparing the book, changes can occur which may affect
the contents. The publishers would welcome notes of any
changes that they find.

Also by Terry Marsh
The Summits of Snowdonia
The Mountains of Wales
The Lake Mountains: Vols 1 & 2
The Pennine Mountains
100 Walks in the French Pyrenees
100 Walks in the French Alps
The Dales Way
A Northern Coast to Coast Walk
50 Classic Walks in the Pennines
Walks with Children in the Lake District: Patterdale

Printed by
Carnmor Print and Design, London Road, Preston

CONTENTS

EXPLANATORY NOTES

Introduction: Questa Walks with Children are intended to introduce young people to hill walking. They range from short, simple river or lakeside ambles, to fairly energetic ascents of fells, sometimes to a considerable height. The walks are not graded, but are intended for groups, with supervised children roughly between the ages of six and fifteen.

Only parents, of course, know just how energetic, determined and resilient their own children are, and so each of the walks gives no more than an indication of the distance to be walked, and the amount of ascent, not necessarily all in one go, you can expect to face. All of the chosen walks have been done with children, and children of all ages have been seen happily plodding along them - they do have remarkable tenacity and boundless energy at times.

But these walks aim to do more than give route descriptions. They aim to educate young and old alike in the interests of the countryside, and the history that surrounds it. So, with each walk a few brief notes tell you what you might find along the way.

Maps: Simple diagrammatic maps accompany each route description. These are based on Harveys Walker's Maps, a specialist map, just for walkers, produced on a waterproof material.

The maps in this book are to scale, either 1:25000 (2½ in to 1 mile~4 cm to 1 km), or 1:40000 (approx. 1½ in to 1 mile~2½ cm to 1 km). These should prove adequate, in good weather conditions, to guide you round the walks, but you are advised always to carry a more detailed and extensive map of the area.

It is recommended that you buy Harveys Walker's Maps if you wish to learn more about the countryside beyond the limited range of our diagrammatic maps. To cover the walks in this book, you will need the maps for North West Lakeland and Western Lakeland. The latter is available in both scales.

Footpaths: Almost all the walks are on public rights of way, permissive paths, or routes which have been used over a period of many years by custom and practice, but any mention of a path does not imply that a right of way exists.

It is unlikely, however, that you will be prevented from following any of the walks mentioned in this book, but you are asked to stick to the paths at all times, especially where they are waymarked, or go through or near farmyards, to be sensitive to the work of the hill farmers, particularly at lambing time, and to keep any dogs you may have with you, under strict and close control at all times.

Equipment: It is important to go well-equipped into the fells, and for everyone this means adequate footwear and waterproof clothing. Small and growing feet will benefit all the more if footwear more substantial than wellington boots or trainers is worn, and will reduce the risk of slipping.

There are rough and wet patches on most of the walks, and for these you will find that modern walking boots with a cleated rubber sole are the best footwear. This remains true even during dry spells in summer: trainers, for example, offer no support to ankles, and while they might be adequate for walking along streets, they cannot cope with steep grassy slopes.

The Lake District, alas, is frequently wet, and a good waterproof should always be carried, along with an extra pullover, cardigan or jacket to compensate for the lower temperatures you will experience as you climb higher, or walk close by the lakes.

Warm trousers, not jeans (which are useless when wet, and offer no protection), are advised, though you don't need expensive walking breeches. Carry extra food and drink, along with your waterproofs and spare clothing, in a small rucsac.

You must always carry a compass, and understand how to use it properly. If you wish to learn more about the skills needed for walking in the hills, you might consider *The Hillwalker's Manual*, by Bill Birkett (Cicerone Press).

Finally, remember to take with you the good sense to turn back if the weather suddenly changes for the worst.

Route Directions: All the walks start from a car park or convenient parking place, but do remember to secure your car against thieves. Keep valuables out of sight, and don't lock animals in the car without adequate ventilation and something to drink.

The directions given in the text are usually right or left in the direction of travel. Sometimes compass directions, east, west, etc. are given. It is on the walks in this book that children can begin learning how to read maps and use a compass. Never let an opportunity to do so go by.

Distances and height gain are measured, and rounded up or down. Distances are 'Total Distance' for the round trip. Height gain is not always continuous, but reflects the many ups and downs you will face.

KEY TO MAPS

The maps in this book are produced at two scales. One is the scale 1:25000, the other, 1:40000. Distances on these maps are represented as follows:

1:25000 (Walks 1, 3, 6, 7, 8, 11, 12, 13, 14, 15, 17)

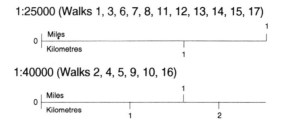

1:40000 (Walks 2, 4, 5, 9, 10, 16)

The following symbols have been used on all maps:

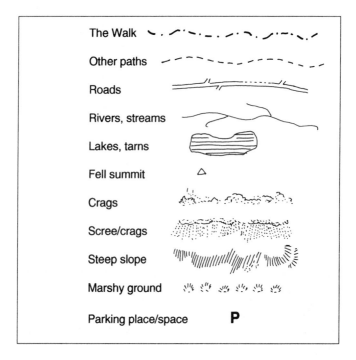

The Walk	
Other paths	
Roads	
Rivers, streams	
Lakes, tarns	
Fell summit	△
Crags	
Scree/crags	
Steep slope	
Marshy ground	
Parking place/space	**P**

BORROWDALE

"any varied landscape, provided it is not marred by hideous...man-made objects...is beautiful...the harmonies of nature are so powerful that no matter what instruments they are played on, in what combinations and at what relative strengths, the result will be pleasing."

Bernard Levin *Hannibal's Footsteps*

Bernard Levin's description is nowhere better exemplified in the Lake District than in Borrowdale (though it was intended as a generality).

Such a view of nature, however, was not one established when the first visitors came to write about the Lake District, but one that had to be fashioned from a background of fear and suspicion. In the Middle Ages everything outside the immediate domain of man was barren and evil, and the mountains and forests the abode of evil spirits, gnomes and trolls. As Norman Nicholson explains in The Lakers: "The Middle Ages had seen the village as a tiny clearing of order among the illimitable wildness of nature; the seventeenth century saw the mountains as the last defiance of disorder among the colonies of civilisation."

That such a view could be held of the beauty we now recognise as Borrowdale is hard to imagine; indeed it is difficult today to think of Borrowdale other than as a most idyllic thoroughfare to its fells and surrounding countryside. Yet it was not always so.

Those who first came to explore the Lakes did so with perceptions coloured by their own view of nature, and that was as much influenced by their social and domestic backgrounds as by their intellectual capabilities.

It was the work of Dr John Brown that led to the first real influx of inquiring visitors. His Description of the Lake and Vale of Keswick (published in 1767), paved the way for Thomas Gray and others, and set the tone for many of the superlative-laden descriptions that were to come: "...at Keswick, you will on one side of the lake, see a rich and beautiful landskip of cultivated fields, rising to the eye in fine inequalities...On the opposite shore, you will find rocks and cliffs of stupendous height, hanging broken over the lake in horrible grandeur, some of them a thousand feet high, the woods climbing up their steep and shaggy sides, where mortal foot never yet approached. On these dreadful heights the eagles build their nests; a variety of water-falls are seen pouring from their summits, and tumbling in vast sheets from rock to rock in rude and terrible magnificence."

Not all of Brown's contemporaries allowed their imaginations to get the better of them, but it was not long before superlatives were to be unleashed on the whole of Lakeland's beauty by the cartload.

Thomas Pennant, usually a reliable observer, paid Borrowdale a fleeting visit on the second of his journeys northwards to Scotland, in 1772. The southern end of Derwentwater, alas, was "a composition of all that is horrible; an immense chasm opens in the midst, whose entrance is divided by a rude conic hill, once topped with a castle, the habitation of the tyrant of the rocks; beyond, a series of broken mountainous crags now patched with snow, soar one above the other, overshadowing the dark winding deeps of Borrowdale."

But it was John Brown's commentaries that lured Thomas Gray northwards, three years before Pennant's second visit, when it was, to quote Molly Lefebure (Cumbrian Discovery), that "The tourist trade, Keswick's major industry today, started inconspicuously...with the quiet arrival of shy Mr Thomas Gray...on 2 October 1769."

Gray was indeed shy, delicate, and unsure of himself, and found himself a little ridiculed by later writers, who protrayed him as so terrified of much of what he saw that he drew the blinds of his chaise. Had that been entirely true he could not have observed: "Gowdar-crag - the rocks at the top deep-cloven perpendicularly, by the rains, hanging loose and nodding forwards."

Nor, beyond the "jaws of Borrowdale" could he have witnessed the "turbulent chaos of mountain behind mountain, rolled in confusion" or that the hills were "clothed all up their steep sides with oak, ash, birch, holly &c...in a place where no soil appears but the staring rock, and where a man could scarce stand upright."

What Gray unwittingly unleashed on the Lakeland world was a great measure of curiosity, and an almost indecent haste among some writers to jump on an early-nineteenth century band wagon. John Housman's Descriptive Tour and Guide to the Lakes, Caves, Mountains and other Natural Curiosities in Cumberland, Westmoreland, Lancashire and a part of the West Riding of Yorkshire observes of Borrowdale: "The verdure of grass, and foliage of trees, now give way to the terrific glare of naked rocks, which overspread the surface with horrid grandeur, and burst out in various huge distorted figures, as if, in this corner of the universe, old Nature had deposited her rubbish during the formation of some happier district."

Although born in Cockermouth, Wordsworth at the age of 17 was sent to Cambridge, but came, with his sister Dorothy to live in Grasmere in 1799. They were followed soon after by their friend Samuel Taylor Coleridge, who settled at Greta Hall, in Keswick, not far from Derwentwater which he found himself unable to resist describing, and in a most eloquent way: "...the vale, the river, and mountain mists, and clouds and sunshine make endless combinations as if heaven and earth were ever talking to each other...", and "...the impetuous gusts from Borrowdale snatch the water up high, and continually at the bottom of the lake it is not distinguishable from snow slanting before the wind - and under this seeming snowdrift the sunshine gleams, and over all the nether half of the Lake it is bright and dazzles, a cauldron of melted silver boiling!"

Many of the early descriptions of the Vale of Keswick, of Derwentwater and the sanctum of Borrowdale scarcely venture beyond Castle Crag, or the Bowder Stone. Gray, the shy, uncertain man, did, so perhaps he should have the last word: "The dale opens about four miles higher, till you come to Seathwaite (where lies the way, mounting to the right, that leads to the wad mines); all farther access is here barred to prying mortals, only there is a little path winding over the fells, and for some weeks of the year passable to the dalesmen; but the mountains know well that these innocent people will not reveal the mysteries of their ancient kingdom."

Thankfully, the modern visitor is spared all these scenes of horror. They haven't changed, but our perceptions have.

Borrowdale is outstandingly beautiful, many of its tree-cloaked sides looking now much as they must have done before man appeared on the scene. Among them this book seeks out its walks with children, and ventures beyond, on to the fells, where the true feeling of mountain land is at its strongest.

All the given routes have been scampered over and along by children of all ages, and will provide pleasure and a sense of achievement that will last a lifetime. Hopefully, too, they will prove the foundations on which a future of wandering among our delectable hills will be built.

WALK 1:
Castlehead, Walla Crag and Friar's Crag

Almost a tour of National Trust properties, this fine circuit of woodlands, crags and lakeshore paths at the northern end of Borrowdale is an excellent introduction both to Keswick and its

Start: Car park, near NT information centre, at Keswick boatlandings. GR 265229
Total Distance: 10 km (6¼ miles)
Height gain: 360m (1180 feet)
Difficulty: Moderate, but the ascent can prove tiring on a warm day.

environs and to the delights of country walking. Not without some effort, the walk nevertheless rewards you with most dramatic scenery, and visits places made popular by the Lake Poets, many of whom found themselves acutely sensitive to the beauty of Borrowdale.

During summer you have the added option of omitting the section that includes a visit to Friar's Crag, by returning to the start on the launch service that operates on Derwentwater, but be sure to check the timetables before you start. Friar's Crag is only a short distance from the start of this walk, so you can always pay it a visit when you get back.

THE WALK:

Leave the car park and turn right to walk up to the roundabout on the main road. Turn right again to the next roundabout at the start of Borrowdale Road.

Go down Borrowdale Road for a few hundred metres/yards to a gate on the left giving access to Castlehead Wood, one of many woodlands in this area owned by the National Trust.

The main path in Castlehead climbs ahead to meet a second

path. Continue, ascending, to the top of this magnificent viewpoint, through woodland comprised of birch, beech and oak.

Benches on the summit are a perfect excuse for a breather, though Castlehead is not a summit to be ticked off and immediately left behind. A viewpoint indicator will help you identify the surrounding fells, towns and villages.

From Castlehead, retrace your steps for 200 metres/yards and

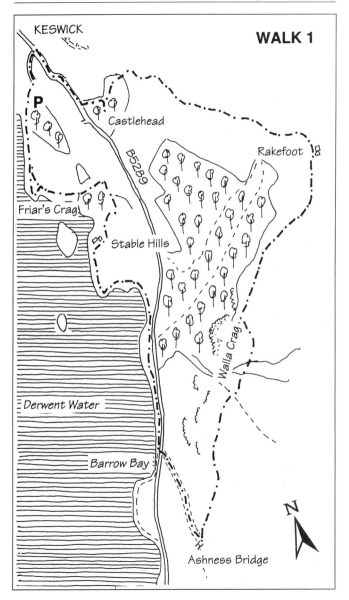

KESWICK

WALK 1

P

Castlehead

B5289

Rakefoot

Friar's Crag

Stable Hills

Walla Crag

Derwent Water

Barrow Bay

N

Ashness Bridge

13

then bear right to reach Springs Road.

Turn right along Springs Road and continue to a farm. Go through the farmyard, and left to follow Brockle Beck. Keep the beck on your left, passing a footbridge, and climbing to a second footbridge beyond which you join another road. Turn right and shortly right again at Rakefoot to re-cross Brockle Beck.

Now simply follow a wall on your right, and cross an intermediate fence to reach the summit of Walla Crag, so concluding the ascent.

Even on a poor day, the views across Derwentwater are magnificent. Across the lake the ridge of Cat Bells is a distinctive feature (Walk 17), backed by the higher summits of the Grasmoor and Grisedale group.

THE WAY BACK:

[The quickest way back, should you need it, is to retrace your steps to Springs Road, and continue down the road to reach Keswick, near the Moot Hall. Before reaching the Moot Hall look for a street on the left (signposted: Borrowdale) that leads down to George Fisher's shop. Go past the shop and down to the lakeshore path.]

Follow the footpath leading away from the summit towards Borrowdale. Cross a stile and go down the path to reach the Watendlath Road at Ashness Bridge.

Do not be tempted to take a path down into Great Wood via Cat Gill, which you will encounter not long after leaving the summit of Walla Crag.

Ashness Bridge is an ancient packhorse bridge, and evidence, along with the numerous upland pathways, that in times gone by there was considerable coming and going across the Borrowdale fells.

From Ashness Bridge, walk down the road to reach the Borrowdale Road at Barrow Bay.

If your timing is right, you can catch a launch from Ashness Gate pier back to Keswick.

Otherwise, follow a permissive path along the lakeshore to Calfclose Bay, where it swings around the northern edge of the bay to reach Stable Hills.

Now the path leaves the shore for a while to enter a small woodland, The Ings, before heading back to the lake and Friar's Crag, close by which there is a monument to John Ruskin. From Friar's Crag it is but a short walk to reach the car park at which you began. On the way you will pass a memorial tablet to Canon Rawnsley, vicar of Great Crosthwaite from 1883-1917.

ALONG THE WAY:
Castlehead village: *In a guide, published in 1819, there is out-*

lined a proposal to construct a village on land around the base of Castlehead. Stones were to be taken from the surrounding rocks, in the process leaving behind lofty waterfalls. "Dwelling-houses, erections of good taste, circular, elliptical, oblong or octagonal, were to be interspersed through the woods. Numerous paths, in many a playful zigzag, were to be made up Wallow Crag, well guarded with handrails and occasionally strewed with flowers, and with fancy seats of stone or wood." The author of the guide, William Green, a surveyor from Manchester who relinquished his profession in favour of becoming a Lakeland artist, based in Ambleside, was convinced that "perfection thus meditated.... would draw forth from every part of the dominion, and concentrate a society, which for its mental elegance, and accomplishments, would be rarely equalled, and this society, though in perpetual change, might be continued as respectable, as refined, by the proper introduction of new arrivals."

The village was never built.

Friar's Crag: Having a close affinity with John Ruskin, Friar's Crag is widely regarded as one of the most outstanding viewpoints in the Lake District, by some, the finest.

A monument close by bears the inscription:

John Ruskin
MDCCCXIX-MDCCCC

The first thing which I remember as an event in my life was being taken by my nurse to the brow of Friar's Crag on Derwentwater

John Ruskin was born in London in 1819, son of a wine merchant, and travelled widely with his parents, visiting Keswick on several occasions. He became a prodigious author, a renowned art critic, essayist, poet and philanthropist. At the age of 52 he bought Brantwood by Coniston Water, where he lived until he died in 1900. He is buried in the churchyard at Coniston.

Canon Rawnsley: Hardwicke Drummond Rawnsley was vicar of Great Crosthwaite, near Keswick, for 34 years. He was a most energetic and industrious man, and instrumental in 1902, in securing the publication of Beatrix Potter's first book, The Tale of Peter Rabbit.

His most notable achievement, however, was the foundation of the National Trust in 1895 with Octavia Hill and Robert Hunter. Rawnsley was Hon. Secretary of the National Trust from its inception until his death in 1920. Appropriately, Friar's Crag, Lords Island and part of Great Wood were given to the Trust in his memory in 1922.

WALK 2:
Around Derwentwater

For runners taking part in the annual half marathon around Derwentwater, among whom I have been known to dawdle, there

> **Start:** The Moot Hall, Keswick. GR 266234
> **Total Distance:** 15 km (9½ miles)
> **Height gain:** Nominal, but many undulations.
> **Difficulty:** Easy walking, but tiring in its later stages. At least one good long break is advised.

comes a point when the wisdom of entering the race comes under close and intensive scrutiny, and armchair notions of trotting round amid delightful scenery tend to lose their comfort. Those prepared to tackle the circuit at a more leisurely pace will, by contrast, discover firstly that they can lop off four miles or so of the route taken by the runners, and secondly that the walk ranks among the finest low level outings in the Lake District.

The length of the walk makes it the longest in this book, but this should deter few. It will, however, be beyond most very young children. Nevertheless, there are a number of opportunities to abridge the walk by returning to Keswick on one of the summer service launches from a number of places around the lake. Timetables are available from any National Park information centre, and are displayed at each of the piers. By this means you can spread the walk over two or more days.

After periods of prolonged rain the section of the walk between Manesty Woods and Lodore, and the headland off Barrow House, is subject to flooding. At these times you will have to extend the walk by following the road to Grange (add 1½ miles), or use the launches between High Brandlehow and Lodore.

THE WALK:

Leave the Moot Hall, and Keswick, along the main road to Cockermouth, a northwesterly direction. Not far out of town the road crosses the River Greta, and immediately afterwards you go left on a footpath signposted to Portinscale. After about 60 metres/yards turn right, through

Portinscale

KESWICK

P

Friar's Crag

Derwent Water

Manesty

B5289

N

WALK 2

a gate and follow a path across two fields to meet a road leading to Portinscale, at which you need to turn left. Cross a suspension bridge spanning the River Derwent and press on down the road to a T-junction, and there take the left branch.

After a little under half a mile the road turns sharply to the left, and later to the right. At the right bend, go left down a lane to the lake (signposted: Launch Pier).

On reaching the lake turn right and go up past Nichol End marina. Now follow an obvious path past Fawe Park and the driveway to Lingholm (gate here) and on through woodland and across fields on a path running between fences. The path eventually reaches another private driveway. When it does, go left and shortly left again, through a small gate to reach Hawse End landing stage.

At the lake turn right and follow the shoreline, cross a stile and follow a fence to a section of boardwalks, continuing then by a pathway through agreeable woodland linking Low and High Brandlehow Piers.

If there is the likelihood of the ground at the southern end of the lake being flooded, it is from High Brandlehow that you will need to catch a launch across the lake to Lodore Pier. Otherwise...

Immediately after High Brandlehow follow the path as it goes right, up steps. At the top, keep ahead to a small gate, beyond which you turn left towards a boathouse. Pass between huts to a gate, and continue along a driveway, turning left on a path opposite a cottage (The Warren).

Follow the path to the shore, and continue along it to a gate in a wall in the middle of Manesty Woods. A short way further on ignore a footpath continuing to Grange, but go left through a gate on to another section of boardwalks that lead to a gated bridge across the River Derwent. Cross the ensuing field to reach Borrowdale Road.

Turn left along the road, past the Lodore Swiss Hotel until, about 200 metres/yards beyond the Kettlewell car park you can turn left, over a stile to a shore path which you can pursue around the headland, meeting the road again near Barrow House youth hostel and Ashness Gate Pier.

Keep on beyond Ashness Gate following the shore path. At Calfclose Bay the path moves away from the road, with Rampsholme Island directly in front of you. Following the shoreline, the path comes to Stable Hills, where a right turn leads along the access road. Soon, however, go left, through a gate into woodland. Cross a footbridge and reach the shore again at another gate. The way is now clear, along the shoreline, to Friar's Crag, beyond which the path runs on into Hope Park, and through a subway. Go up the ensuing street, turn left at the top, and soon you will reach the Moot Hall once more.

ALONG THE WAY:

Islands: *The many islands on Derwentwater have played a significant part in local history. Records show that Lord's Island was the seat of the Radcliffe family, noted in 1539 by Leland as 'the Head Place' of the family. It still remained in 1653. described as 'all that capital messuage or mansion house called the Isle'. By 1709 it and its gardens were described as destroyed, and Lord's Island has rather lapsed back to its former state, and there is a tradition that the old Moot House in Keswick was partly built from the stones of the Radcliffe mansion in 1695.*

There is evidence of a bloomery on Rampsholme Island, but nothing now to show of the cell of Saint Herbert who once inhabited St Herbert's Island as a hermitage, and about whom Wordsworth penned 'The Hermit of Derwent Water'.

On Derwent Isle the German miners of Elizabethan Keswick, originally imported to work the mine of the Newlands valley, ran all manner of businesses, including a "brewhouse, a windmill, a pigeon-house, garden and orchard, and a drying-floor for corn."

Moot Hall, Keswick: *The present Moot Hall, built in 1813 on the site of an earlier building, was until fairly recent times used as the town hall. The word 'moot' means 'to argue or discuss', so the Moot Hall was a place of discussion.*

Barrow House: *Built by an eccentric local, Joseph Pocklington, Barrow House now sees service as a youth hostel. Formerly Pocklington had lived on Derwent Isle, but began building this imposing mansion on 26 March 1787. The final cost of the house and grounds was recorded as £1,655 3s 6¾d!*

Pocklington, who was known as Lord Pocky was responsible for annual regattas on Derwent Water. Described as a man of ebullient fancy who never understood the concept of restraint, he built several Picturesque extravaganzas on his island, including a Druid's Circle. Further down the valley, at the Bowder Stone, Pocklington constructed a small cottage and installed an old woman as a resident guide.

WALK 3:
King's How and the Bowder Stone

The section of Borrowdale south of the village of Grange is arguably the finest and most attractive part of the whole dale; it is

certainly one of the most popular reaches, and scenically of the highest order. Here the valley narrows dramatically into a ravine appropriately described as the Jaws of Borrowdale. On either side of the valley are two out-

Start: Bowder Stone car park. GR 253169
Total Distance: 5½ km (3½ miles)
Height gain: 340m (1100 feet)
Difficulty: Easy; some uphill work

standing viewpoints: one, Castle Crag is visited in Walks 8 and 12, the other, King's How, by this walk.

THE WALK:

Leave the car park and turn right, following a pedestrian footpath along the road. After about 400 metres/yards turn right, over a stile (signposted: Grange Fell) and follow the ensuing path.

In a short while, go right at a junction, continue to a gate in a wall. Beyond the gate, ignore a stile on the left, and go ahead to cross a stream, then climbing steeply through pleasant woodland, following a line of cairns.

At the top of the path you meet a fence. Ignore the stile, but continue right, alongside the fence. Shortly, the path moves away from the fence, climbs a little more, and then returns to ascend to a small

cairn. A short distance away is a memorial stone, and the summit of King's How.

THE WAY BACK:

From the memorial, return to the small cairn, and turn right, descending steeply to a stile across a fence. Keep ahead, and cross a wall by a ladder stile, then following a clear path that runs on, downhill, towards Rosthwaite in the valley below.

When you reach the edge of a conifer plantation, turn right (do not go into the plantation) and follow a path, right, to a wall. Keep alongside the wall and at a corner go through a gate, following a path steeply down through

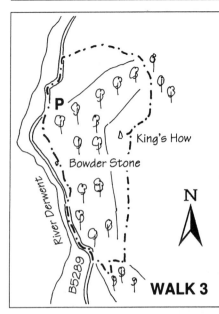

*PEACE
HERE MAY ALL
BEINGS GATHER
STRENGTH AND
FIND IN SCENES OF
BEAUTIFUL NATURE A
CAUSE FOR GRATI-
TUDE AND LOVE TO
GOD GIVING THEM
COURAGE AND
VIGOUR TO CARRY
ON HIS WILL*

The area around the Bowder Stone and King's How were purchased by the National Trust in 1910, the year the King died. His sister, Louise, was Duchess of Argyll, and died, at the age of 91, in 1939.

Bowder Stone: *No one seems quite sure whether the Bowder Stone fell from the crags above, or was left by a retreating glacier, an erratic, though the latter is the more probable. The name comes from the Middle English 'bulder-stan', meaning a large boulder.*

Nearby, is a small cottage built by Joseph Pocklington, at the end of the eighteenth-century, as a home for a guide. In the base of the boulder is a small hole, also the responsibility of Pocklington, who made it so that visitors could shake hands through it with their guide. The stone is reputed to weigh about 2,000 tons.

woodland to reach the valley road. Turn right, along the road for 550 metres/yards.

At a signposted path, leave the road for a path that takes you to the Bowder Stone.

When you have thoroughly inspected the Bowder Stone and the nearby cottage, press on to return easily to the car park.

ALONG THE WAY:

King's How: *The memorial on King's How bears the inscription:*

IN LOVING MEMORY OF
KING EDWARD VII
GRANGE FELL IS DEDICATED BY
HIS SISTER
LOUISE
AS A SANCTUARY OF REST AND

WALK 4:
Ashness Bridge to Watendlath

In medieval times the lands of Borrowdale, formerly owned by Alice de Rumelli, heiress of the Barony of Allerdale, were held by the monks of Furness Abbey, while "Watendlath and the fells thereof" had been given to Fountains Abbey in 1195. When Henry VIII dissolved the monasteries, between 1536 and 1539, he granted the Watendlath lands to Richard Graham of Netherby, who held the grant of land until 1606 when the entire Graham clan was deported to Ireland for their part in Border disturbances. The name, Watendlath, comes from Old Norse, vatns endi, meaning the 'end of the lake'.

Start: Car park just above Ashness Bridge. GR 270196
Total Distance: 7 km (4½ miles)
Height gain: 90m (295 feet)
Difficulty: Easy; a little road walking, most of which can be avoided.

The setting of Watendlath today many regard as idyllic, though a visit in the depths of winter might change your mind. On the 8th August 1800 the Wordsworths "walked over the mountains by Wattenlath", an excursion described by Dorothy in The Grasmere Journals *as "A most enchanting walk. Wattenlath a heavenly scene."*

Ashness Bridge is an old packhorse bridge made notable as a foreground to a most attractive view of Derwent Water and the Skiddaw fells beyond. This walk, which involves walking up to Watendlath and back again, links Ashness Bridge and Watendlath, and fashions a course through pleasant woodland. Refreshments at Watendlath, and the opportunity to explore, will occasion a lengthy delay before you set off down again.

THE WALK:

Leave the car park and set off beside the road, heading south, and gently uphill, the road flanked by birch and sessile oak. Before long you have the chance to leave the road for a moment and approach one of the most dramatic views in Lakeland, directly above the Lodore Swiss Hotel.

The sudden drop here is not one at which children should be encouraged to rush headlong, nor is it a place for anyone suffering from vertigo.

Having safely retreated from the view only a little more walking beside the road is necessary before you can leave it for a delightful romp through woodland, and, later, beside Watendlath Beck. The path rises and falls, and meanders about a little, but this only serves to heighten the charm, and is a pleasant prelude to the suddenness of the white buildings of Watendlath that appear through the trees.

A few small cascades lead you to the packhorse bridge at the entrance to the hamlet.

THE WAY BACK:

The simplest return is back the way you came, a prospect not in the least diminished by treading familiar ground.

The only realistic alternative is to cross the southern shoulder of Grange Fell, by a path climbing easily from Watendlath, southwest along the line of Bowdergate Gill, and to descend to Rosthwaite, from where a bus may be caught back to Barrow Bay. To do this, you need first to be sure of the timetable for the buses, which are available from the information centre in the Moot Hall in Keswick.

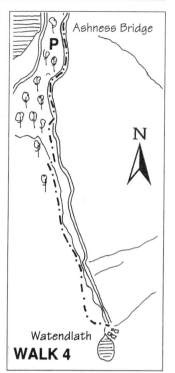

ALONG THE WAY:

Watendlath: *In the* Herries Chronicles *Hugh Walpole made Watendlath the home of his heroine Judith Paris, and for a while there was a danger that Judith Paris might do to Watendlath, what Kathy, in Wuthering Heights, did to the Haworth Moors, or Lorna Doone to Exmoor. Thankfully, Watendlath, in its cradle in the mountains, needs no such support; in autumn it is a corner of Heaven burnished gold.*

WALK 5:
High Seat

High Seat is the highest point along the broad wedge of ground sandwiched between Borrowdale on the west and Thirlmere on the east. With a mere five or six feet more of height (two metres

Start: Watendlath. GR 276163
Total Distance: 6 km (3½ miles)
Height gain: 340m (1115 feet)
Difficulty: Moderate; the initial uphill start is loose in places, and the middle section invaribaly wet. Care is needed on the descent.

or so) it would achieve 2000 feet, a figure that some people feel is needed to award 'mountain' status. Such a distinction is a daft one, and unlikely to perturb sensible walkers.

Sadly, a good stretch of the ridge rising to High Seat is wet and boggy, and were it not for needing the good ankle support provided by walking boots on the climb up from Watendlath, I would recommend wellies for this one! - wellington boots, alas, don't give you the support you need.

Set against this soggy dilemma you have breathtaking views, especially of the Helvellyn and Fairfield massifs to the east, and the messy conditions underfoot are always a good test of temperament. If you can find a day following a period of dry weather, progress will not be such a problem.

The walk starts from Watendlath, but the possibility exists of beginning from Ashness Bridge, and then descending directly to Watendlath from High Seat, from there using the descent of Walk 4 to return to Ashness Bridge: a note on that possibility is given at the end of this walk.

THE WALK:

Leave the car park at Watendlath and turn right to gain the obvious zigzagging path up the adjacent fellside. The initial steepness soon eases, and is followed by an expanse of wet ground across which the path is not always clear.

For this reason, the walk is not recommended in poor visibility: in any event, the view is the compensation for poor conditions underfoot.

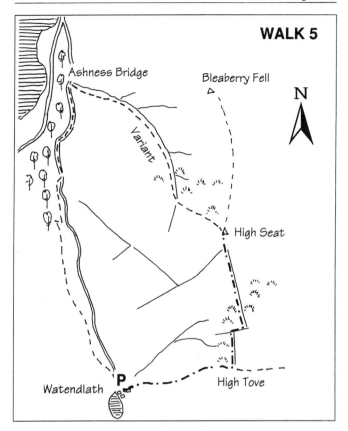

If you now continue in an easterly direction, still roughly following your original course, you will intersect a fenceline near the top of a minor rise called High Tove.

This is the point where the view significantly improves, and does so both east and west, looking back to the high central block of Lakeland, in which *Great Gable features prominently.*

Now head north (left) from High Tove, following the fenceline, and doing your best to avoid the worst of the conditions. The fence twice turns through ninety degrees before heading directly for the rise of High Seat.

The fence ends about 200

metres/yards from High Seat, which is now easily reached.

The top of the fell is marked by a trig pillar, though whether this or a nearby rocky outcrop is the highest point is something you can mull over as you enjoy the view, and lunch.

THE WAY BACK:

The only way back to Watendlath is to retrace your outward steps, remembering to change direction when you reach High Tove, and then exercising caution as you descend the zigzag path back to Watendlath.

VARIATION:

With a modest amount of extra effort you can vastly raise the quality of this walk by beginning from Ashness Bridge. This will increase the height gain to 445 metres (1460 feet), and the total distance to 9 kilometres (5½ miles). This is a little more demanding, but fully stocked with interest and outstanding views.

From Ashness Bridge go along the road for a short distance until you have passed the nearby building, and then turn left to follow an obvious path alongside a wall, climbing with Ashness Gill on your left. Higher up, the gill closes to a narrow ravine, containing splendid waterfalls (take care here, where the path passes close to the edge of the ravine), and beyond reaches the heathery northern slopes of High Seat. You can follow a fenceline to the top of High Seat, or take a shortcut, if you wish.

The return journey heads for High Tove, as described above, following the fence, and then descending, with care, to Watendlath, where you connect with Walk 4, following this down, alongside Watendlath Beck, past the Lodore 'surprise' view, and down through the woodland, back to Ashness Bridge.

Packhorse Bridges

Many of the old stone bridges of Lakeland, like those at Watendlath and Ashness, were almost certainly packhorse bridges, probably built between 1660 and 1760, at a time when packhorses were still in general use as a means of transport over difficult terrain. Their existence today tells of a time when trade routes across and around the fells were commonplace.

WALK 6:
Brund Fell

Brund Fell is the highest point of a far more expansive hill, Grange Fell. Compared with loftier Lakeland heights, Grange Fell is of modest proportions, yet it is of exquisite loveliness, as if the beauty earmarked for the bleakness of north Pennine moorlands has been hijacked and crammed into the tiny compass of Grange Fell.

Start: Rosthwaite. GR 259148
Total Distance: 5½ km (3½ miles)
Height gain: 480m (1575 feet)
Difficulty: Quite strenuous, and rough in places. The descent from King's How is steep and requires care.

Walk 3 visited King's How, which is part of the larger Grange Fell, and this walk, too, takes the opportunity to embrace King's How, for good measure.

Rarely will you see the heavy-booted, serious-faced brigade of fellwalkers on Grange Fell; if you do, you'll be looking at a connoisseur of the sublime.

The top of the fell is a knobbly arrangement of rocky tors within the embrace of carpet heather, on which young adventurers can practice a little rock scrambling. On the minus side, the top of the fell can be confusing in poor visibility, so a clear day is recommended.

THE WALK:

Leave Rosthwaite as if heading along the road to Keswick, but just as you leave the village turn right at the entrance to Hazelbank Hotel on a bridleway (signposted: Stonethwaite and Watendlath) that leads to an arched footbridge over Stonethwaite Beck.

Ignore the turning, alongside the beck, to Stonethwaite, and continue instead on an enclosed path that soon leads you out on to open fell and a steady pull through gates and across a slab bridge spanning a small stream, to a gate near the top of the pass, at a spot called Puddingstone Bank.

The on-going path from the top of the pass continues down to Watendlath. With time in hand you might think about dropping

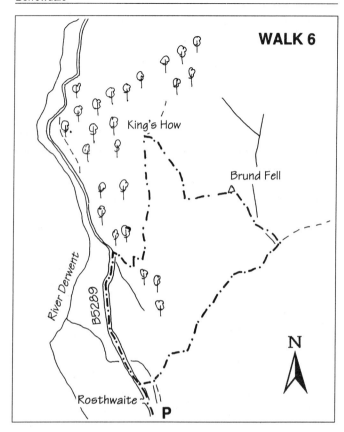

WALK 6

King's How

Brund Fell

River Derwent

B5289

Rosthwaite **P**

N

down to this enchanting hamlet, where refreshments may be found. This will add about 2 km (1¼ miles) and a little reascent.

At the top of the pass go through a gate, then head northwards beside a wall to a ladder stile. Cross the stile and continue climbing to the top of Brund Fell.

From such a fine vantage point the view is immense and rewarding, extending on a clear day as far as the Solway Firth and the mountains of the Galloway region of southern Scotland.

THE WAY BACK:

The return journey, other than reversing the ascent, continues across the knobbly top of

Grange Fell to King's How. Across the valley Castle Crag is especially prominent.

From Brund Fell walk towards Castle Crag until you meet a distinct footpath, and here turn right, crossing two stiles before finally pulling on to King's How. *(see Walk 3 for information on the memorial on King's How).*

From the top of King's How walk southwards, in the direction of Rosthwaite, following a line of cairns and descending steep zigzags on which young children will need control. Pass through a wall gap into woodland, and press on down, through gates to reach the valley road. Here turn left to return to Rosthwaite.

Old Stone Walls

No visitor to Lakeland can escape without noticing the proliferation of stone walls, mile upon mile of zigzagging, soaring, meandering impositions that appear unsuccessfully to contain the fellsides, or rocket up the hills with no apparent purpose other than to reach the top.

All northern counties have their dry stone walls, but the Lake District seems to have more than its fair share. The usual claim for their existence is that they sprouted from the enclosure laws which came into being during the eighteenth-century, but their is a likelihood that many originated from the days when the monasteries flourished and bred sheep. Certainly, Wordsworth (1770-1850) gives the impression in his writing that the stone walls had been in existence for some time.

The enclosure laws were the most common method of converting medieval open fields into more manageable arrangements, enclosed by hedges, and later by walls. But many of the walls that are found in Lakeland pre-date these laws, perhaps being even as much as 1,000 years old. Many follow the boundaries of parishes, or large estates.

Whatever the truth of their origin, it is certain all the building had been completed more than 100 years ago, only repair work has gone on since, and a skilled job it is, too.

WALK 7:
Dock Tarn

Dock Tarn lies tucked away on a rise of high ground south of the hamlet of Watendlath. From Watendlath, most walkers make for the larger, and rather more wildly set, Blea Tarn, but a splendid walk to Dock Tarn is possible from Rosthwaite. Dock Tarn forms part of an outstanding, but complex, arrangement of rocky tors, heather banks, wooded slopes, and general confusion, described by Wainwright as "a beautiful labyrinth, a joy to the explorer".

Start: Rosthwaite. GR 259148
Total Distance: 6 km (3¾ miles)
Height gain: 340m (1115 feet)
Difficulty: Apart from the ascent, none. Not advised in poor visibility

On a clear day there is ample opportunity for young legs to explore the many undulations of this fell, which tends to assume the overall name, Great Crag. The top of the fell has an abundance of sheltered spots to pass the time, musing, dreaming, reflecting on the meaning of life, but not for a moment regretting the impulse that sent you this way. With scarcely any ingenuity you can easily clamber to the top of Great Crag, rising with distinction above the carpet of heather, at its best in late August and early September.

THE WALK:
Leave Rosthwaite in the direction of Keswick, but soon turn right at the entrance to Hazelbank Hotel on a track (signposted: Stonethwaite and Watendlath). Having crossed Stonethwaite Beck by an arched bridge turn right on a signposted footpath heading for Stonethwaite. The on-going path, partly enclosed, runs alongside the beck, and later becomes a field path with gates, leading to Stonethwaite Bridge.

At Stonethwaite Bridge the path is signposted for Grasmere via Greenup Edge. Continue along it, keeping Stonethwaite Beck always on your right, and, after the second gate beyond Stonethwaite Bridge, locate a path going left, slanting across a field and rising into woodland.

The short section between Rosthwaite and the point where

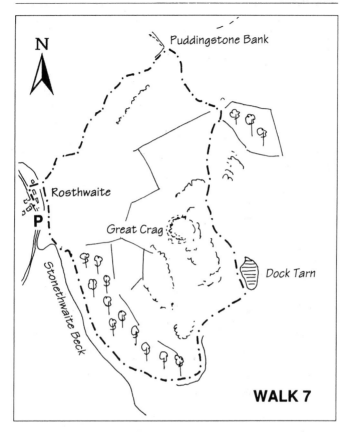

WALK 7

you left the valley path, is part of a superb long distance walk, the *Northern Coast to Coast Walk,* which extends from St Bees on the west coast of Cumbria, to Robin Hood's Bay, 178 miles away, on the North Sea Coast.

The rising path crosses a wall, before climbing through the woodland in a series of zigzags before breaking free of the trees,

and out on to heather fell top. Follow the path, right, through two walls, one in better condition than the other, and climb easily to reach Dock Tarn.

Great Crag lies to the west of the tarn, and is easily reached across heather slopes.

THE WAY BACK:
Continue on the path that passes

along Dock Tarn's western shoreline. When it forks, take the left branch, and walk on to reach a path (used in Walk 6), linking Rosthwaite and Watendlath.

It is, of course, perfectly feasible to take the right branch when the path forks, and to descend to Watendlath, where refreshments are available. A return by the Rosthwaite path is then easily made.

From the top of the path, Puddingstone Bank, turn left, through a gate and start descending, crossing a side stream by a slab bridge, before going down through gates to a track leading down to the valley road at Hazelbank.

The Borrowdale Woods

While revisiting the walks contained in this book, I spent some time perched on the flanks of Cat Bells and Maiden Moor, taking in the scenery. Most notable, apart from everything being exactly where you would want it, were the great wooded valley sides, that looked, to my inexpert eyes at least, just as I would imagine Borrowdale, and much of England, would have looked two or three thousand years ago.

Borrowdale probably has far more woodland composed of native trees than any other Lakeland valley. I say 'composed' of native trees, because, of course, the ancient forests have long since been cleared for timber and charcoal production during centuries gone by. Today, what you see is known as semi-natural woodland, formed by replanting native species, and as a result coming very close to reproducing the original, natural woodland character of the district.

Many of the Borrowdale woods are hanging on steep, well-drained slopes, based on the underlying rocks of the Borrowdale Volcanic Series. Most of the trees you see are a mix of sessile oak, sycamore, rowan, holly, hazel, birch, with alder and willow especially finding favourable conditions in the valley bottom, near the River Derwent. In a few places, Johnny's Wood is a good example, you will find larch has been introduced.

WALK 8:
Castle Crag from Rosthwaite

There is plenty of evidence that the people of Borrowdale, in days before history was recorded, felt the need to protect themselves

Start: Rosthwaite. GR 259148
Total Distance: 4 km (2½ miles)
Height gain: 200m (655 feet)
Difficulty: Steep and rough in places. The final pull on to Castle Crag is sensational.

against some enemy, even though the nature of the enemy is rather obscure. Perhaps the clearest indication lies in the ruins of the fortification they built on Castle Crag, about 2000 years ago. About this hill fort two things are certain among many uncertainties: one that it existed at the time of the Romans, from the presence of Roman pottery fragments found there, the other that it still existed around the tenth-century, or later, when the Norsemen came to the dale: they called the dale 'Borgar-dalr', or 'Borgarárdalr', the valley of the fort.

THE WALK:

Just opposite the general shop in Rosthwaite a narrow road is signposted for Grange. Follow this, pass through a farm, and follow a lane down to reach the River Derwent.

When you reach the river, if it isn't too heavily swollen, you can cross it by stepping stones, though very young children may find this too daunting. If you are unable to cross at this point, simply follow the river, right, until you meet New Bridge.

Cross the bridge, turn right and go through a gate on the left on to a path that climbs the fellside beyond. You cross a stile, and must then keep an eye open for a gate in a wall towards the skyline as you look at Castle Crag.

Go through the gate and head for Castle Crag, passing through a gap in a wall to a ladder stile* (see Variation below). Once you have crossed the stile, you reach the top of Castle Crag by a steep and slaty path on which care is needed, especially if it is wet.

VARIATION:

From New Bridge, turn left and cross the first small footbridge.

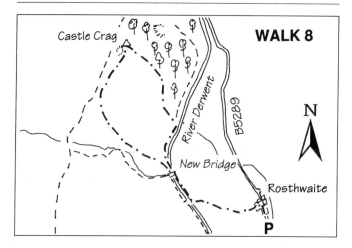

Then cross the stile on your right and walk beside the beck, and across two stiles.

Follow the path as it passes round a small hill and climbs steadily to meet a wall. Ignore the path to Scale Close Coppice and Seatoller, but turn right, still climbing.

After a gate, go right, over a stile, and cross Tongue Gill. Follow the path until just before reaching Castle Crag you can take a narrow path on your right, across a low wall, and on beside a fence to the ladder stile* mentioned above.

Now you can finish the climb to the top of the Crag by the steep and slaty path - take care!

The summit of Castle Crag is a neat arrangement of rock outcrops into which quarrying has carved unsightly holes. Keep young children in check (and always in sight) here, since the path passes close by the edge of the summit quarry.

The view down Borrowdale towards Keswick and Derwent Water is outstanding, and Castle Crag one of the surest ways of gaining a true and lasting impression of the qualities for which the Lake District is famed.

THE WAY BACK:

To return to Rosthwaite, retreat to the ladder stile, from where a path descends to a gate and steeply down through woodland to another path linking Rosthwaite and Grange. Turn right and follow the path back to New Bridge, retracing your steps from there.

ALONG THE WAY:
Castle Crag: *Castle Crag is in the ownership of the National Trust, having been given to the Trust in 1920 by Sir William Hamer and his family in memory of his son John Hamer, 2nd Lieut. 6th KSLI (killed in action in 1918) and of ten other men of Borrowdale, also killed in the First World War.*

Castle Crag

"From the top of Castlecrag in Borrowdale, there is a most astonishing view of the lake and vale of Keswick, spread out to the north in the most picturesque manner...a beautiful mixture of villages, houses, cots and farms, standing round the skirts of Skiddaw, which rises in the grandest manner from a verdant base and closes this prospect in the noblest stile of nature's true sublime. From the summit of the rock the views are so singularly great and pleasing that they ought never to be omitted...This truly secreted spot is completely surrounded by the most horrid, romantic mountains that are in this region of wonders; and whoever omits this *coup d'oeil* hath probably seen nothing equal to it."

Thomas West
A Guide to the Lakes (1778)

West was writing his *Guide* at a time when the first tourists were coming to the Lake District in search of the awe-inspiring as much as the picturesque, and it was not unusual to read of them seeking such diverse qualities as beauty, horror and vastness all at the same time.

WALK 9:
Langstrathdale

Langstrathdale lies behind the Borrowdale Fells, sandwiched between Glaramara and High Raise, a region of amazing beauty and ruggedness that makes you feel good. From the upper end of Langstrath, you can cross over the Stake Pass and into Langdale. Such a walk is a long one, but immensely satisfying.

Start: Rosthwaite. GR 259148
Total Distance: 12 km (7½ miles)
Height gain: 140m (460 feet)
Difficulty: Fairly easy; rough and stony underfoot

The lower part of the valley, from Stonethwaite is steep-sided and wooded, and as H H Symonds comments in his classic book Walking in the Lake District, *first published in 1933: "full of colour and projecting rock...a lonely valley, greatly varied...with that charm of hidden resources which comes to any valley where a sharp knee-bend hides a lower half from the upper." The sharp knee-bend is a sudden change in direction from Stonethwaite into Langstrath proper, a route this walk takes.*

There are no heights to ascend on this walk, just rough and stony tracks to contend with, and a few stream crossings. After that you are on your own, miles from anywhere, or so it seems, and your only burden is having to cope with the unending joy of walking in one of Lakeland's finest crannies.

THE WALK:
Leave Rosthwaite along the road, as if heading for Keswick, but soon turn right, near the Hazelbank Hotel on a track (signposted: Stonethwaite and Watendlath). Cross the arched bridge spanning Stonethwaite Beck and turn right to follow the beck.

At varying distances from Stonethwaite Beck, the path moves on through gates as you cross fields and the occasional stream. Finally, you approach Stonethwaite Bridge, with the hamlet of Stonethwaite on the far side of the beck.

Ignore the bridge, and press on through two more gates.

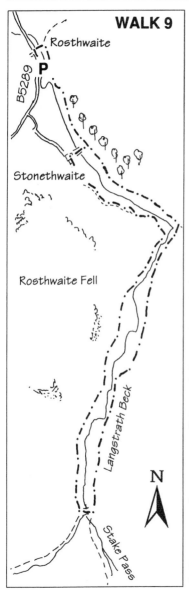

WALK 9

Rosthwaite

P

B5289

Stonethwaite

Rosthwaite Fell

Langstrath Beck

N

Stake Pass

Up to this point the route has been shared with Walk 7 to Dock Tarn, which here departs across a field on the left. It is also part of the Northern Coast to Coast Walk, and the Cumbria Way, which tells you something of its pedigree.

Along this stretch, the view into the valley is dominated by the cliffs of Eagle Crag, while away to your right you can pick out the white dash of Taylorgill Force beneath Base Brown, with the fells of Green Gable and Lingmell beyond.

Carry on, over two small footbridges to reach the first of many cascades, Galleny Force, product of the combined forces of Langstrath Beck and Greenup Gill.

Just above the confluence of the two streams, you need to cross Greenup Gill by a narrow wooden bridge, preceded by a stile and succeeded by a gate.

A short way along Langstrath Beck yet more delightful falls await. If you need to shorten the walk, you will soon be able to cross Langstrath Beck by a bridge, rejoining the full route on the other side.

Now start heading deep into Langstrath, meeting the occasional gate and stile, until, just below the confluence with Stake Beck you can cross Langstrath Beck by a footbridge.

This is a far as the walk goes from your starting point, and the setting is a particularly fine and wild one in which to call a lunch halt.

Here in this far corner of Langstrath, fashioned years ago by glaciers, the countless streams come and go with the rainfall, at one moment invisible, at the next, great white foaming slashes down the hillsides - soggy going underfoot, but an impressive sight.

THE WAY BACK:

Follow a good path that runs on down the west (true left) bank of Langstrath Beck passing beneath the craggy slopes of Stonethwaite Fell and Rosthwaite Fell. Across the valley are the big cliffs of Sergeant and Heron Crags, and Eagle Crag.

Near the confluence with Greenup Gill a footbridge on the right is the point at which the shorter version of this walk joins the longer route.

Stay on a good track, heading towards Stonethwaite either by keeping to the old road, or by branching right and going through a camp site. Either way brings you to the hamlet.

Pass through Stonethwaite and turn right at the telephone and post box to cross Stonethwaite Bridge.

Once back across Stonethwaite Beck, turn left, and retrace your steps to Rosthwaite.

ALONG THE WAY:

Eagle Crag: *The naming of many Lakeland features is often of obscure origin, but in Eagle Crag there is clear evidence of a time when eagles flew freely over Lakeland fells before they were persecuted to extinction. Thankfully, in recent years, the eagles have returned to the Lake District.*

Stake Pass: *The monks used to use Stake Pass to carry wool into Langdale, while ore came back from Eskdale, via the Ore Gap and the Stake, to a bloomery on Smithymire Island where Langstrath Beck and Greenup Gill meet.*

Stonethwaite Lake: *Though there is little evidence of it today, the long neck of Stonethwaite, as far as the meeting of Greenup Gill and Langstrath Beck, once formed a lake. A collection of moraines, up to 30 feet high, near Rosthwaite effectively cut off Stonethwaite from the main glacial trough of the valley, impounding water behind them. Even now, the beck has to wriggle a little to find its way into the main valley.*

WALK 10:
High Raise

The summit of High Raise would win no accolades in a perfect mountain competition, being largely bare and without

> **Start:** Rosthwaite. GR 259148
> **Total Distance:** 13 km (8 miles)
> **Height gain:** 670m (2200 feet)
> **Difficulty:** Fairly strenuous in places, some steep ascents, but with ample opportunity for rest halts. Not suitable for very young children.

real distinction, though it does try to mollify this deficiency by casting a fine ridge northwards brimming with crags that have brought the attentions of the rock climbing fraternity over the years. But the approach from Rosthwaite is a fine companion, and renders palatable that which might

otherwise be left. By contrast, the confines of Stonethwaite Beck and Greenup Gill are everything they should be, resplendently craggy and bouldery, with a host of fine waterfalls and bright green fellsides to enliven progress.

For young walkers keen to learn the skills of map reading and navigation this visit to High Raise is well ordained. As far as Greenup Edge, the route follows the course of an old packhorse route, probably used by the monks at Furness Abbey.

The return route described here is a simple retracing of one's outward steps, but I have given a variant finish down steep grassy slopes into Langstrath: these are tiring, pathless, and should not be attempted in wet conditions or poor visibility.

THE WALK:

Begin by following Walk 9 as far as the point where Greenup Gill and Langstrath Beck meet below the gaze of Eagle Crag (see pages 36 and 37). Do not cross Greenup Gill, but continue instead along its eastern flank, the path gradually rising all the

time, and the display of waterfalls improving almost with every step.

As you climb, so the scenery becomes more dramatic, more forbidding. On the way you pass a boulder on which there is a memorial plaque to a walker who "died in peace under the shelter of this rock in the early hours of Sunday 8th January 1939"

For a while the paths flirts with mini-cascades that crash over boulders, before leaving them behind. As the sound of white water dies away you reach a large corrie, quite unsuspected from below, and formed by glacial action, as you can see from the large number of moraines scattered beneath the prow of Lining Crag.

You approach Lining Crag on an ascending path, passing around it on an improved pathway, finally to conclude the greater part of the uphill work.

The view from the top of Lining Crag is stupendous, and sudden, but well worth a moment's pause.

Once you are above Lining Crag, follow a cairned path across boggy ground to reach Greenup Edge. As you meet the remains of a fenceline (or earlier on a clear day) go right, ascending first to Low White Stones, and then by a grassy trod on to High Raise, the top of which is named High White Stones, and marked by a large cairn and trig pillar.

The top of the fell is largely featureless, but the panorama is immense, embracing almost every major Lakeland summit as well as the Pennines, the Irish Sea and the Solway Firth. From an instructional point of view, High Raise is a perfect place to teach children how to set the map, and how to relate what they see on the ground to the various features on the map.

THE WAY BACK:

The easiest return is to retrace your steps. This will pose no problem other than as you approach the top of Lining Crag, when you must take care to locate the improved section of pathway, down to the right. Once this is safely passed, you can happily tramp down the valley.

VARIANT FINISH:

[Not recommended in wet conditions or poor visibility - you need to see where you are going.]

From the summit trig you must take a line just north of west, starting down fairly easy grassy slopes that become much steeper lower down. As the ground steepens you will see the confluence of Langstrath Beck and Stake Beck, and this is your objective. Take it very easy going down this stretch.

When you reach the valley bottom, you may cross Langstrath Beck or not, to suit your purpose, either following the return route described in Walk 9, or reversing its outward route. Either side of the stream will bring you back to Greenup Gill, from where a return may be made to Rosthwaite.

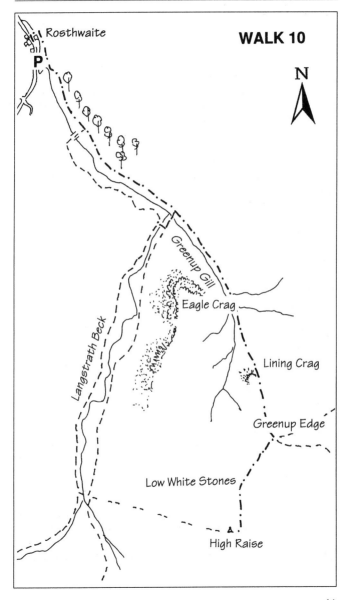

WALK 10

N

Rosthwaite

P

Greenup Gill

Langstrath Beck

Eagle Crag

Lining Crag

Greenup Edge

Low White Stones

High Raise

WALK 11:
Bessyboot and Tarn at Leaves

Bessyboot is a fine little summit at the northern end of the long ridge that reaches its highest point in Glaramara. This is an area where

Start: Seatoller car park.
GR 245138
Total Distance: 6 km (3½ miles)
Height gain: 440m (1445 feet)
Difficulty: Quite a long, steep pull to Tarn at Leaves, but otherwise moderate.

confusion often arises over which bit of this very knobbly ridge is which. Bessyboot is a prominent rise just north of delightfully-named Tarn at Leaves, while Rosthwaite Fell, of which Bessyboot probably forms part, lies to the south, and is rather higher. To make matters worse, the top of Rosthwaite Fell is sometimes known as Rosthwaite Cam or as Cam Crag. Wainwright, who studied these matters rather more assiduously than most before putting pen to paper, gives the name Rosthwaite Fell to Bessyboot, and separately identifies Rosthwaite Cam and Cam Crag as two independent eminences. Confusing, isn't it?

THE WALK:
Leave the car park at Seatoller and turn left down the road, following it round until your reach Strands Bridge. Just over the bridge go right on a back road that leads ultimately to Seathwaite, but shortly leave it, on the left, for a path used by walkers heading for Glaramara.

Follow this path, climbing steadily, until, after a gate and near a sheepfold, you can cross Combe Gill, and leave the Glaramara path to begin climbing steep grassy slopes to the left of the conspicuous red ravine of Rottenstone Gill.

After what seems like an eternity, the gradient eases, and you find Tarn at Leaves lying in a neat hollow. Bessyboot, a knobbly top knot, lies a few hundred metres/yards to the north, and is easily reached from the tarn. Its protective ring of low crags is easily breached.

THE WAY BACK:
Simply to retrace your steps, is the safest way back; but take care descending those grassy

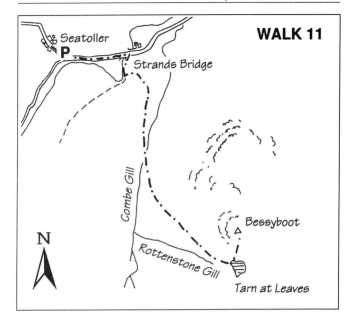

slopes down into Combe Gill, which can be slippery when wet.

ALONG THE WAY:

Seatoller: *Sharing with Seathwaite the distinction of being the wettest place in Lakeland, Seatoller lies at the foot of the Honister Pass. Its name, which derives from the Old Norse 'saetr', a summer pasture, or shieling, does not appear in print until 1563, but it is unlikely that such a prominent location was not in regular use long before then.*

Norse influences

You have only to look at the map to see the extent of Norse influence on the place-names of Lakeland: *dalr*, a valley; *fjall*, a hill; *gil*, a ravine; *bekkr*, stream, *tjörn*, a small lake, none of them far removed from the present day, dale, fell, gill, beck or tarn littered across the maps of the district.

WALK 12:
Castle Crag from Seatoller

Castle Crag was visited as part of Walk 8, from Rosthwaite, but this circular walk approaches Borrowdale's most distinctive feature from the south, stops off for a while to visit Castle Crag, and then continues northwards to reach the River Derwent, which it then largely follows back to Seatoller. With care, this is a walk you can tackle in almost any summer weather conditions, or can be left until the bracken turns gold in autumn, when you may have more of the walk to yourself.

Start: Seatoller car park. GR 245138
Total Distance: 7½ km (5 miles)
Height gain: 170m (555 feet)
Difficulty: Easy walking; care needed on the ascent of Castle Crag, especially in wet conditions

For much of the way the walk follows an old packhorse trail, and passes through what is, for many visitors, the most attractive part of Lakeland. It is a fairly simple route on which children could usefully practice map reading, and learn to identify distant places on the map.

Quite possibly formed as a result of volcanic activity, Castle Crag is really an extension of Low Scawdel, itself part of the much bulkier High Spy. There is no doubting its prominence, it stands as a formidable barrier to what lies beyond around which both man and river have been obliged to chart a course, formidably independent and rugged, and only marred by what man has done to it.

The quarry near the summit of the crag is evident enough; on the steep slopes above the Derwent there is more, a series of quarries and caves, now largely concealed by shrubbery, but not a place for young minds to explore...or, for that matter, old ones.

THE WALK:
Leave the car park and turn right to enter Seatoller village. Pass the National Park Information Centre at Dalehead Barn (worth a visit), and continue out of the village on the road bound for Honister and Buttermere.

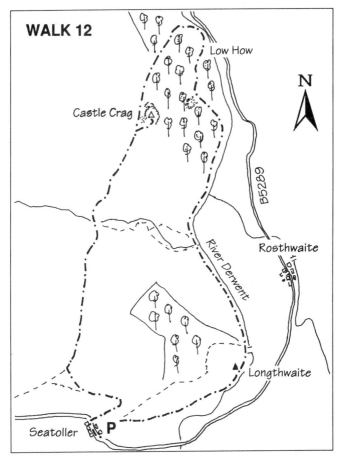

WALK 12

Low How

Castle Crag

N

B5289

River Derwent

Rosthwaite

Longthwaite

Seatoller **P**

Soon after leaving the village, abandon the road at a gate on the right giving on to a well-graded track that climbs easily, and swings left past a stand of oak trees and Scots pine.

This is the old road linking the quarries at Honister with Borrowdale. In 1819, Seatoller had but five houses. A hundred years later that had more than trebled, and by 1946 there were twenty four. The cottages were built for workmen at the quarries, now they serve a different trade, that of tourism.

Shortly, you leave this old road, bearing right and uphill to a gate near a wall junction. Go through the gate, and turn right, now on a good track heading northwards and before long crossing Tongue Gill by a foot-bridge.

In the higher reaches of Tongue Gill (visited by Walk 16) lie the Rigghead Quarries; dangerous places to wander about in, but fascinating to visit and study. The track from Tongue Gill onwards to Grange was formerly constructed to serve the quarries; it now serves the purposes of walkers most admirably.

Continue along the track until almost upon Castle Crag, an enormous spill of scree betraying the quarry above. Leave the track at this point on a path bearing right to a wall. Cross the wall, beyond which a memorial seat provides a moment's rest, and continue to cross another wall by an awkward stile.

Turn right once across the stile and follow a slaty path that works a way upwards in zigzags to the top of Castle Crag.

Near the top, where the path passes very close to the edge of the summit quarry, keep young children under close control.

Return to rejoin the main track by the same route, there turning right and continuing northwards through Dalt Wood.

When the path descends towards the River Derwent, follow it round below Low How, always taking the most obvious route through what is some of the most charming woodland and lakeside scenery in the Lake District. The path climbs to some disused slate quarries before continuing through High Hows Wood.

Eventually, you break free of the woodland cover and follow a clear path the New Bridge.

Do not cross the bridge, but keep on to Longthwaite youth hostel, beyond which the path runs on easily, finally to return to the car park at Seatoller.

ALONG THE WAY:

Memorial seat: *The seat found just on starting the ascent of Castle Crag bears a memorial plaque: "The land surrounding the summit of Castle Crag was given to the Nation in memory of Sir William Hamer, MA, MD, FRCP by his wife Agnes, whom this seat commemorates. 1939."*

Longthwaite youth hostel: *This purpose-built hostel, in Canadian red cedar, was opened in 1939, to which an extension was added in 1969, and is ideally placed for all of the walks in this book.*

WALK 13:
Taylorgill Force

Few of the early visitors to the Lake District ventured further down Borrowdale than the Bowder Stone. Those that turned back at this 'wonder' therefore missed the savage scenery that lay beyond, though the presence of wad mines was known when Gray came to Borrowdale in 1769, largely ahead of the rest.

For the study of glacial action there are few places to better these far reaches of the valley which originate in the central massif around Scafell Pike and Great Gable, where snow must have accumulated in large quantities during the Ice Age, thus assuring the valleys of a plentiful supply of new ice. Beyond Seathwaite and Stockley Bridge there is an extensive area of hummocks formed by a retreating glacier, while the side valleys of Gillercomb and Styhead Gill have clearly been cut off by the enormous force of a main valley glacier.

Start: Seathwaite Farm. GR 235122
Total Distance: 5 km (3 miles)
Height gain: 285m (935 feet)
Difficulty: Moderate; a little easy scrambling is needed. Rough and wet underfoot.

The valley of Styhead Gill is visited in this walk, lying at some considerable height above the main Grains Gill route, and as a result sending its water down in a fine series of waterfalls, Taylorgill Force. At the end of the last Ice Age, about 8-9000 BC, much of the valley as far as Seathwaite would have been flooded, forming a long lost lake.

For many walkers, Taylorgill Force is merely a white dash on the landscape en route to somewhere else. But the falls are quite splendid, and deserve to be visited for their own merit. The route given here makes a simple loop around the falls, almost reaching to Styhead Tarn before retreating by way of Stockley Bridge.

Some modest scrambling, of no great difficulty, occurs on the approach to the falls; for a very short distance young children will need a watchful eye.

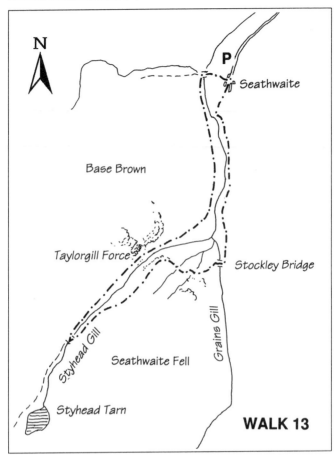

N

Base Brown

Taylorgill Force

Stockley Bridge

Styhead Gill

Grains Gill

Seathwaite Fell

Styhead Tarn

P

Seathwaite

WALK 13

THE WALK:

The walk begins at the very end of the motorable road into Borrowdale, at Seathwaite Farm. Parking is possible off road here, but the place is a popular base for trips into the surrounding mountains, so don't expect to turn up late and find a parking spot.

Walk towards the farm, and turn right through an arch in the buildings. Continue to cross the River Derwent by a stout bridge and, with Sour Milk Gill tumbling down above you from unseen Gillercomb, go left at the first gate to tackle a stretch of boggy ground.

Keep going on a fair path beneath the towering slopes of Base Brown, gradually turning the base of the mountain until you start to ascend through a downfall of boulders.

A short way further on and up you meet, of all things, a gate, hard pressed against a rock wall. Rock faces rise above you here, and a little scrambling, of the easiest kind, is needed to make progress: children will love it.

In only a few minutes the rocks are passed, and your are descending to meet the great mare's tail of Taylorgill Force, screened from walkers on the opposite bank by a stand of trees.

There are few occasions when Taylorgill Force fails to put on a display, but take care not to let young children approach too closely.

The path continues above the falls, and starts heading into the inner sanctum of Sty Head and its circle of bold and craggy fells - Great Gable, Lingmell, Scafell Pike, Broad Crag and Great End. Follow it, taking care as you cross wet slabs and on the rough path, until you meet a bridge spanning Styhead Gill, and here cross to begin the return journey.

With time to spare you could delay crossing the bridge, and continue for a few more minutes to reach Styhead Tarn, a beautiful setting in which to enjoy lunch, but plagued by sheep that know what to expect from walker's sacks.

THE WAY BACK:

Cross the bridge and turn left, following a rough and stony path back towards the trees that shelter Taylorgill Force.

Descend along the top edge of the trees on a broad path that lower down crosses a minor stream or two.

Continue down through low rock outcrops to approach a wall, crossing it by a gate to reach Stockley Bridge.

Keep on the path over the bridge, and follow it easily back to Seathwaite.

In times of spate the river at this point is a fascinating and formidable sight.

ALONG THE WAY:

Stockley Bridge: *Borrowdale suffers badly from the effects of heavy rainfall, and on 13th August 1966 considerable damage was done. In just one hour more than four inches of rain fell. The streams rose rapidly as every depression down the fellsides sent its water into the valley. Massive boulders were forced down the main channel above Seathwaite, and the lovely arched bridge at Stockley completely wrecked.*

WALK 14:
Gillercomb and Base Brown

Base Brown is in many ways a frontier: it marks the end of the 'poetic' beauty that typifies the main thrust of the Borrowdale valley, replacing it with a different, but no less appealing beauty, that of rugged nature at its best. Sadly, most walkers simply pass by Base Brown on the way to higher fells, but it is a splendid objective in

Start: Seathwaite Farm.
GR 235122
Total Distance: 5 km (3 miles)
Height gain: 515m (1690 feet)
Difficulty: Moderate; the climb into Gillercomb can be tiring, and the subsequent path through the valley sometimes wet.

itself, an impressive, shapely, craggy mass from which to view the surrounding heights, and on which you are likely to have far less company than on neighbouring heights. Along with its companions, Brandreth and Grey Knotts, across Gillercomb, Base Brown is like a stubby finger projecting from the fist of Great and Green Gable, and often omitted from a walk to those two higher fells, when it could so easily be included.

This walk approaches Base Brown, by the easiest route, through Gillercomb, a place that geologists and eager young minds, will find fascinating. As you climb it is clearly evident that Gillercomb is a classic hanging valley, and that the floor of it, now wet and boggy, must have housed a small tarn not too long ago. This splendid amphitheatre is frown upon by numerous crags, some of which have attracted the attentions of rock climbers, and which offer enterprising routes in winter conditions.

THE WALK:

Leave Seathwaite through the arch in the buildings on the right and go along the ensuing track to cross the River Derwent by a footbridge.

Once across the bridge, continue ahead with the splendid cascade of Sour Milk Gill foaming down above you.

Soon you cross a wall on your left by a stile to follow a path leading upwards to the Seathwaite Slabs, a popular,

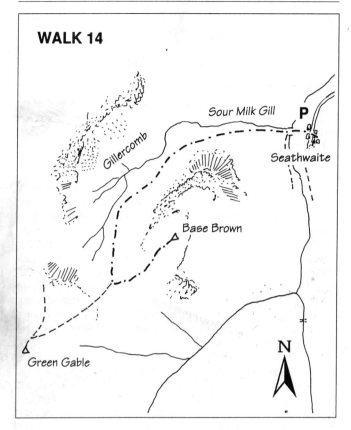

WALK 14

Sour Milk Gill

P

Gillercomb

Seathwaite

Base Brown

Green Gable

N

easy-angled rock slab suitable for novice rock climbers. Indeed, you will find yourself faced with a little easy scrambling, but it should deter no one.

Above the slabs the path works a way up to a gap in a wall, and provides you with some fine views of Sour Milk .

At the top of Sour Milk Gill you cross a band of grey-green rock, *known to geologists as andesitic tuff. The darker fragments in it are tell-tale signs of a violent explosive eruption, one that would have occurred during the formation of the Lake District, millions of years ago.*

At this dramatic entrance to the hanging valley above you also encounter small humps, or moraines, formed when the

51

glacier that once filled Gillercomb, and which gouged out the valley, finally lost its impetus on meeting the main valley glacier, and simply dumped its burden of boulders and boulder debris. It is this barrier which would have impounded the former lake behind it, and which even today hinders the otherwise natural drainage of the valley.

Beyond the valley lip take a path heading into the valley, which is level for a good part of the way, but then climbs fairly steeply to a broad grassy col between Base Brown, on your left, and Green Gable, directly ahead. At the col, turn left on an indistinct and wet path to reach the summit of Base Brown. After so much cragginess below, the top of Base Brown, grassy with only a sprinkling of boulders, comes as a surprise.

To some extent the view is restricted by higher fells, but to the south you have a splendid view of the highest mountains of all, ranging from Great End to Scafell Pike and Scafell.

THE WAY BACK:

The safest retreat is back the way you came. The eastern slopes of Base Brown are notoriously steep and loose, and though there is a way down the north ridge of Base Brown it is not suitable for very young children and involves negotiating a few scattered rock outcrops that can easily deflect you on to steeper ground.

OPTIONAL EXTRA:

If you are feeling especially fit and the day is fine and clear, you can think of continuing to Green Gable.

This involves returning to the col, from which you would descend to Gillercomb, but continuing on a well-worn path that clambers upwards to meet a path coming in from your right, from Honister. When you do, turn left along it to climb to the top of Green Gable. The view, especially of Great Gable, is quite outstanding, and worth the effort. This addition, however, will add 2½ km (1½ miles) of walking, and 195m (640 feet) of height gain, so be sure you want to take it on.

Take care on retreating from Green Gable that you don't miss the turning into the head of Gillercomb.

ALONG THE WAY:

Plumbago mine: *If you look northwards as you climb beside Sour Milk Gill, you might pick out on the fellside (GR 232127) some mining spoil. This marks the site of a unique deposit of plumbago, or graphite, and was the origin of the local pencil industry.*

WALK 15:
Styhead Tarn and Sprinkling Tarn

When first I came to the Lake District I was fascinated by the variety of strange-sounding names: Sprinkling Tarn was but one place I just had to visit to discover quite what it was that sprinkled. I'm not convinced I ever found out, but I did discover that this central part of the region is notorious for its rainfall.

> **Start:** Seathwaite. GR 235122
> **Total Distance:** 9 km (6 miles)
> **Height gain:** 540m (1770 feet)
> **Difficulty:** Moderate, with short sections of uphill work, and a sustained downhill stretch. Rough and rocky underfoot throughout; boots are recommended.

In the mid-1980s I indulged in endurance mountain marathons to raise money for charity. Early one June morning I had ascended Ben Nevis in Scotland, Britain's highest mountain, in magical conditions, the early morning mist evaporating above me as I climbed. From the summit, beneath an almost clear sky I could pick out my next objective, Ben Macdui (second highest mountain) many, many miles away. Several hours later I and my entourage reached the Lake District, bound for an ascent of Scafell and Scafell Pike. It seemed as though it was the day for topping up the lakes and tarns, as non-stop torrential rain lashed the mountainsides. A group of soggy Glaswegians huddled behind a rock at Styhead were amazed to hear that the Bens were in perfect condition, and, rather more sceptically, that I had climbed them both earlier that day.

But no amount of rain can erode the sheer majesty of Styhead, encircled by a ring of massive mountains, awesome in their power. Even today, a shiver runs down my spine whenever I perch on my favourite spot beside nearby Sprinkling Tarn and gaze upon the graceful symmetry of Great Gable, as I rest beneath the towering crags of Great End.

This outstanding circuit leads you into the very heart of mountain Lakeland. It is a fairly energetic walk, but well worth the perseverance, especially if undertaken in spring or autumn, when the colours of the fellsides are at their most vibrant, and the hills are just a touch less crowded.

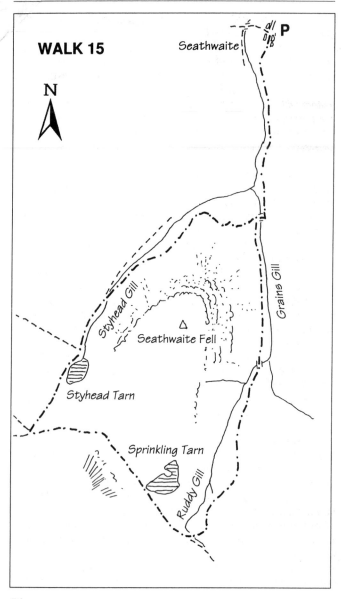

THE WALK:

Seathwaite is about as far south as you can drive and still remain technically in Borrowdale. For generations the Edmondson family have lived here, plying visitors with refreshments and, in more recent times, fresh fish from their own trout farm. It has always been a major launch pad for the fells of central Lakeland, and is ideally placed to gain access into this magnificent mountain country.

Leave Seathwaite by heading south past the farm buildings, and soon cross a minor stream by a wooden plank bridge. Shortly, you pass through a gate and reach more open country-side, where the combined forces of Styhead Gill and Grains Gill , now the River Derwent, cast aside massive granite boulders as if they were marbles.

Ahead the dark cliffs are those of Seathwaite Fell, quite an awkward summit to reach, and best achieved from the shores of Sprinkling Tarn. To your left the formidable slopes of Glaramara lead the eye to far off Esk Hause, while on your right, the lesser, but no less impressive, fellside of Base Brown terminates a broad spur of the Gables massif.

Continue then along the course of the River Derwent, the path undulating a little before it finally reaches Stockley Bridge, an ancient packhorse bridge, just upstream of the point where the two gills combine.

Cross the bridge and go through a gate in a wall. Ignore the path going left along the wall, but walk away from the gate on a prominent path teasing a way through low outcrops of rock to cross a feeder stream issuing from the slopes of Seathwaite Fell above.

Soon the path climbs beside a stand of birch and larch through which you can pick out the white dash of Taylorgill Force (Walk 13), one of Lakeland's most splendid waterfalls.

The climb beside the woodland is quite a pull, but thankfully short-lived. Soon you are back on less steep ground, as a rocky path leads on parallel to Styhead Gill, later crossing it by a wooden bridge.

As you walk into this hidden sanctum, so the magnificence of the surrounding mountains unfolds. Seathwaite Fell gives ground to Great End, beyond which rises Broad Crag and the highest summit in England, Scafell Pike. Directly ahead you are faced by the sternness of Lingmell, dwarfed by the immense bulk of appropriately-named Great Gable to your right. Directly above, a scree runnel between Great Gable and Green Gable, named Aaron Slack, is reputedly a passageway used by Stone Age man as he trekked from the axe factories of Langdale to the coastal plains.

Once across Styhead Gill you soon come upon Styhead Tarn, a perfect place for a rest, nestling in a small hollow, though surprisingly it was not fashioned by a corrie glacier, scientific study revealing in the tarn sediments a continuous record of late-glacial vegetation of grasses, sedges and mosses.

Moving on beyond Styhead Tarn, Styhead Pass itself is soon reached.

The Pass is a major mountain crossroads, but predominantly a high mountain link between the valleys of Borrowdale and Wasdale. There is arguably no better non-summit location in the whole of Lakeland than the rocks of Styhead Pass.

With your back to Great Gable, Seathwaite Fell lies half left, and Great End rather more to the right. Between the two, a good path rises to the very edge of Sprinkling Tarn. Almost anywhere along its shores would make an ideal spot for lunch, if you haven't already eaten it. But the rocks that surround the tarn make a perfect rocky playground for energetic young legs.

THE WAY BACK:

Return to the main path and continue climbing. The path ultimately goes to Esk Hause and over into the Langdale valley.

Before long a deep, red-sided ravine appears on the left, the red coming from extensive outcropping of haematite. A short distance further on you can descend to cross the top of the ravine - it is named Ruddy Gill - to reach its far bank.

The subsequent path descending into Borrowdale was for many years quite unstable and dangerous, but repair work in the early 1990s has substantially restored stability. Even so, this is no place for youngsters to charge about headlong, and care is needed until you are a long way down into the valley.

Of course, what you simply cannot do on terrain such as this is to walk and look at the view at the same time. If you do want to take it all in, then stop for a moment, close mouths, and open eyes and ears. To heighten your perceptions of the nature that surrounds you, close your eyes as well, and listen, very intently.

In time you cross the stream by a stout footbridge, beyond which the path leads down to the wall near Stockley Bridge. The final stage of the walk retraces your steps from there.

On a warm day the pools upstream of Stockley Bridge make splendid foot baths - a small towel carried in anticipation is a non-essential, but utilitarian, item of hill-walking equipment.

WALK 16:
The High Spy ridge

As you drive into Borrowdale from the north, the fells that await your attention seem to lie back with a relaxed, welcoming air, but by the time you reach Grange the scenery, that so easily intimidated the early travellers to the region, has dramatically changed. Great sweeping fellsides, dotted with crags and boulders rise behind the village, sporting a variety of names - Nitting Haws, High White Rake, Low Scawdel, Lobstone Band Door - and providing what must be one of the most lasting impressions of Lakeland's rugged countenance.

Start: Grange. Limited parking just over the bridge, near chapel, at GR 254175, or roadside parking on B5289 at GR 256176.
Total Distance: 10½ km (6½ miles)
Height gain: 600m (1970 feet)
Difficulty: Moderate: initial uphill work is easily broken into sections, and the main ridge is easy walking on a good path. The descent by the disused quarries can be slippery when wet - young children must be kept under control at all times here, and must not be allowed to enter any of the open mine levels.

Essentially, all these many-named eminences form the easterly flank of one long mountain, High Spy, though its northerly end seeks independence and bears the name, Maiden Moor. The complete traverse of the ridge, once you are on it, is outstanding. Easy walking abounds, with views, notably east across Borrowdale and west across the delightful Newlands valley, that are among the finest in Lakeland.

Gaining the ridge, at Maiden Moor, involves a little energetic uphill work, but there are plenty of valid as well as opportunistic spots at which to halt for a breather and to admire the view. Once the ridge is crossed, this walk provides an interesting return to the start by visiting the area of former quarrying activity at Rigghead on High Scawdell, before returning to the valley and passing through the awesome 'Jaws of Borrowdale'.

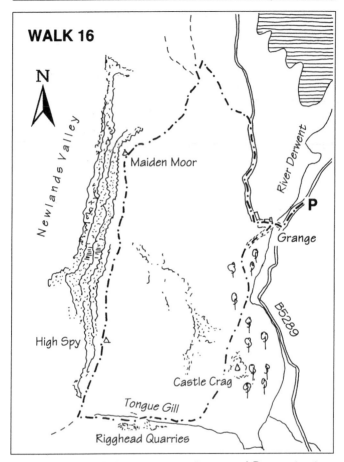

THE WALK:

Walk through the village of Grange, noting as you do a signposted path on the left - this is the way by which you will return. Continue pleasantly along the road, but take care with small children, the road is part of a popular motorised route around Derwentwater.

As you pass Manesty, take a broad track leaving the road on the left, and ascending gently. When the track forks, take the left branch, and climb in stages to Hause Gate, the broad grassy col between Cat Bells and Maiden Moor.

When you reach Hause Gate, a short diversion to look down on the Newlands valley, and pause for rest, is well worthwhile.

Returning to the Hause, take a clear path climbing the obvious shoulder to the south. The highest point of this, just off the main path, is Maiden Moor, and a fine spot from which to recover from the ascent, which is now virtually all over.

The on-going route continues in easy style to the rocky top of High Spy, crowned by a large cairn.

This is excellent walking; on your left the fells fall to Borrowdale, while to the right, they plummet ruggedly to the wild upper reaches of the Newlands valley, scene of much mining activity, especially during the time of Elizabeth I.

THE WAY BACK:

The way back, other than by simply retracing one's steps, lies in continuing across the top of High Spy, and gradually descending towards Dalehead Tarn, which comes into view ahead and to the right.

Do not continue all the way to the tarn, but part way down the slope from High Spy look for a small cairn off to the left on the edge of a fairly level stretch of ground. This marks the start of a short expanse of wet ground, but leads to a step stile across a fence at the top of Tongue Gill.

This short section holds the only potential in this walk for confusion, so a little extra care is needed in checking you have the correct line.

Once at the head of Tongue Gill, press on ahead, led on by cairns, soon to encounter the first of the quarry workings. The path through the quarries is prominent, but the slaty conditions underfoot can be slippery when wet.

Do not allow children to enter the open, horizontal shafts (adits), which are invariably wet and potentially dangerous.

Half way down Tongue Gill the path crosses the beck. Go with it, and keep descending to meet a horizontal track, linking Grange with Seatoller. This is a bridleway, and part of the Allerdale Ramble, one of Lakeland's longer distance walks.

All you need do now is to go left and follow this path back to Grange.

On the way you will pass Castle Crag, a rocky volcanic wedge in the Jaws of Borrowdale (visited both by Walks 8 and 12) and go through delightful riverside glades that are a keystone of Borrowdale's beauty.

WALK 17:
Cat Bells ridge

Not only is the ascent of Cat Bells a popular walk, it is probably the most popular walk within reasonable distance of Keswick. For such a small mountain, it attracts a disproportionate share of attention, and has been the first step on the fell-walking ladder for many a visitor to Lakeland.

Start: Small quarry, and limited parking at GR 249197
Total Distance: 5.5 km (3½ miles)
Height gain: 385 m (1265 feet)
Difficulty: The ascent to the ridge is energetic, but otherwise undemanding, and the crossing of Cat Bells nowhere difficult, though very young children will need restraining on the rocky descent from the summit.

It is not only the ease of ascent that attracts everyone to Cat Bells, indeed some might argue that 'ease' is a very subjective term in the context of Cat Bells, but every step of the way is accompanied by outstanding views in which the familiar and not-so-familiar constantly change their appearance as height is gained or lost. The view across Derwentwater, to Skiddaw, Lonscale Fell, Blencathra, Bleaberry Fell and the Dodds is breathtaking, and a more than adequate reason for numerous halts to take it in, while (coincidentally, of course) regaining the breath the view took away in the first place.

Cat Bells is for everyone; a deservedly popular mountain, a familiar and distinguished sight, especially seen across Derwentwater, with a perfect blend of easy and uphill walking. Even so, it doesn't please everyone: one young plum-voiced component of a school party met with while revisiting Cat Bells for this book was heard to remark in an over-loud voice: "This is the first time I've climbed a mountain. I can't see what anyone finds so fascinating about it. I certainly shan't be doing this again." What his immediate colleagues muttered about both him and his point of view is, alas, unprintable - but essentially they shared a significantly differing opinion.

THE WALK:

From the quarry take a steadily rising path southwards, that climbs gradually away from the road until it is high above the woodlands of Manesty Park and Brackenburn, the sometime home of Sir Hugh Walpole.

Stay on the path, in spite of any tempting shortcuts, until you reach the edge of the woodland by a combination both of the path descending slightly and the woodland rising to meet it. From a wall corner, take a clear path climbing steeply to join the main line of ascent from Manesty. On reaching the main path, turn right, and climb, occasionally alongside a fence, finishing in zigzags to reach Hause Gate, the broad grassy col between Cat Bells and the higher fell to the south.

Go across the col for a splendid view down into Yewthwaite Gill and the Newlands valley.

Return to the col and ascend northwards on a broad path, up a slight rise, before you reach the base of Cat Bells' rocky little summit.

There are numerous spots all around the summit in which to seclude oneself, and enjoy a well-earned break. The view is marvellous: to the north the

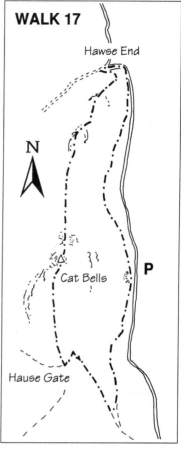

WALK 17

Hawse End

N

Cat Bells

P

Hause Gate

grey, shaly slopes of Skiddaw form a splendid backdrop for the town of Keswick, to its left the blue expanse of Bassenthwaite Lake. Further right, you can see the distinctive profile of Blencathra. Looking west, the view is of the grand circle of fells of Coledale - Eel

Crags, Sail and Grisedale Pike.

TO CONTINUE:

When suitably recovered, press on across the top of Cat Bells. The path down is nowhere in doubt, but has a few minor rock outcrops to contend with, and these are flanked by grassy slopes that in places could intimidate, and might be slippery if wet. Keep very young children under close control here, at least until you reach the broad col that lies at the foot of Cat Bells' main summit.

The next minor summit along the ridge, sometimes called Brandlehow, brings more moments of delightful walking, and leads to another steepish descent, this time twisting about to ease the gradient. At its end, you step on to the road at Hawse End.

Turn right, ignore the road descending to the left, and go right, following the road back to Grange for a short distance, before leaving it by a bridleway (on the right), that rises gently across the flanks of the summits you have just traversed, and passes through stands of gorse that in spring and summer are heavy with the scent of cinnamon.

The path, in an unhurried and delightful way, unerringly returns you to the quarry car park.

ALONG THE WAY:

Cat Bells: *It seems certain that Cat Bells takes its name from the wild cat, that used to inhabit many English forests until the eighteenth-century; the last wild cat in England was killed in North umberland in 1853, though they still populate remote parts of Scotland in small numbers.*

Formerly, 'Cat' would have been rendered in Old English as 'Catt', while 'Bells' derives from the Middle English word 'belde', giving a combined meaning of 'the den of the wild cat'.

Brackenburn: *Overlooked during the early part of this walk, Brackenburn used to be the home of Sir Hugh Walpole (1884-1941), English novelist, born in Auckland, New Zealand. He stayed at Brackenburn between 1923, when he bought it, until his death. His collection of works known as 'The Herries Chronicle' (1930-1933) was set in and around Borrowdale, and his skill in evoking atmosphere ensured that the work did much to popularise the region.*

Walpole died on the 1 June 1941, and is buried in the grounds of St John's Church, Keswick.

As you walk around the base of Cat Bells, you may find a commemorative tablet and bench erected by one of Walpole's friends.

GENERAL INFORMATION
AND
USEFUL ADDRESSES

LAKE DISTRICT NATIONAL PARK

The Lake District National Park is the local government body established in 1951 to preserve and enhance the beauty of the area, and to promote quiet public enjoyment and understanding. At 885 square miles, the Lake District is the largest of the national parks throughout England and Wales.

Contrary to popular belief, much of the land in the national park is privately-owned, and the National Park Authority works closely with landowners to ensure that the 1800 miles of footpath is accessible both to the local population, and the annual influx of visitors.

Visitor information about any part of the national park, together with an accommodation booking service, informative exhibitions, free information, and a comprehensive range of guidebooks and maps, are available from the National Park Tourist Information Centres, situated on Lake Road, Keswick, and at Seatoller Barn. The centres are open daily from 10.00 am to 5.00 pm from 1 April to 3 November (or thereabouts), with some extension of opening hours during the summer months.

Lake District National Park Office, Murley Moss,
Oxenholme Road, KENDAL, Cumbria, LA9 7RL
Tel 0539 724555: Fax 0539 740822

CUMBRIA TOURIST BOARD

The Cumbria Tourist Board exists to guide the development of the tourism industry in Cumbria, to bring economic, social and environment benefits to the region. It operates a Tourist Information Centre in the Moot Hall, Keswick (Tel: 07687 72645), which has a free local accommodation booking service. Open usually from 10.00 am to 4.00 pm, with extensions in summer.

Cumbria Tourist Board, Ashleigh, Holly Road,
WINDERMERE, Cumbria, LA23 2AQ
Tel 05394 44444

WHERE TO STAY

The scope for overnight accommodation anywhere in the Lake District is enormous. All the towns and villages within travelling distance of Borrowdale - Keswick, Portinscale, Penrith, Threlkeld and Ambleside - have plentiful bed and breakfast accommodation ranging from private houses to hotels and guest houses of a high standard, while virtually every village and many of the farms have some bed and breakfast accommodation. Wherever you go, you will be assured of a warm and friendly welcome.

There are many camping and caravan sites, and these are shown on the various maps that are available. Members of the Youth Hostels Association will find youth hostels at Ambleside, Derwentwater, Grasmere (Butterlip How and Thorney How), Honister Hause, Keswick, Longthwaite and Thirlmere conveniently situated for the walks contained in this guide. Those who are not members may like to join. Write to:

Youth Hostels Association National Office
Trevelyan House, 8 St Stephen's Hill,
ST ALBANS, Hertfordshire, AL1 2DY

or

YHA Northern England Regional Office
PO Box 11, MATLOCK, Derbyshire

LAKE DISTRICT WEATHER

In the Lake District the weather is often very much a law unto itself. The months from April until July tend to be the driest of the year, while autumn quite often proves an excellent time of year for walking. By the time September and October arrive, you could encounter the occasional flurry of snow, or a chilling wind, but you are just as likely to have prolonged periods of calm and a serene stillness for which the Lake District is renowned. You can get local weather reports from a few places. Weather bulletins are usually posted at national park car parks and tourist information centres. Or you can ring -

Lake District Weather Service
0768 775757